EARTH

How to Use Your SD-X Reader with This Book

This highly informative book introduces you and your child to the Earth in a new interactive format. You can read the book and study the rich illustrations, but a touch of the SD-X Reader adds in-depth audio information, word definitions, and learning games to the pictures and text.

1. Press the Power button to turn the SD-X Reader on or off. The LED will light up when the SD-X Reader is on.

2. Touch the volume buttons found on this page or on the Table of Contents page in this book to adjust the volume.

3. Throughout the book, words in this color provide additional information when they're touched with the SD-X Reader. Objects on the page may also play additional audio.

4. At the top left corner of each spread, you'll see circles like these: ● ● Touch a circle to start a learning game or quiz. Touch the same circle again to stop playing the game. Touch another circle to start another learning game or quiz.

5. Some learning games will ask you to use Ⓣ Ⓕ buttons or Ⓐ Ⓑ buttons to answer. For other learning games, touch objects on the page to answer.

6. When you've answered all the questions in a learning game, you'll hear your score.

7. After two minutes of inactivity, the SD-X Reader will beep and go to sleep.

8. If the batteries are low, the SD-X Reader will beep twice and the LED will start blinking. Replace the batteries by following the instructions on the next page. The SD-X Reader uses two AAA batteries.

9. To use headphones or earbuds, plug them into the headphone jack on the bottom of the SD-X Reader.

CHANGE THE VOLUME WITH THESE BUTTONS:

UP   DOWN

Battery Information
Includes two replaceable AAA batteries (UM-4 or LR03).

Battery Installation
1. Open battery door with small screwdriver.
2. Install new batteries according to +/- polarity. If batteries are not installed properly, the device will not function.
3. Replace battery door; secure with small screw.

Battery Safety
Batteries must be replaced by adults only. Properly dispose of used batteries. See battery manufacturer for disposal recommendations. Do not mix alkaline, standard (carbon-zinc), or rechargeable (nickel-cadmium) batteries. Do not mix old and new batteries. Only recommended batteries of the same or equivalent type should be used. Remove weakened or dead batteries. Never short-circuit the supply terminals. Non-rechargeable batteries are not to be recharged. Do not use rechargeable batteries. If batteries are swallowed, in the USA, promptly see a doctor and have the doctor phone 1-202-625-3333 collect. In other countries, have the doctor call your local poison control center. This product uses 2 AAA batteries (2 X 1.5V = 3.0 V). Use batteries of the same or equivalent type as recommended. The supply terminals are not to be short-circuited. Batteries should be changed when sounds mix, distort, or become otherwise unintelligible as batteries weaken. The electrostatic discharge may interfere with the sound module. If this occurs, please simply restart the sound module by pressing any key.

In Europe, the dustbin symbol indicates that batteries, rechargeable batteries, button cells, battery packs, and similar materials must not be discarded in household waste. Batteries containing hazardous substances are harmful to the environment and to health. Please help to protect the environment from health risks by telling your children to dispose of batteries properly and by taking batteries to local collection points. Batteries handled in this manner are safely recycled.

Warning: Changes or modifications to this unit not expressly approved by the party responsible for compliance could void the user's authority to operate the equipment.

NOTE: This equipment has been tested and found to comply with the limits for a Class B digital device, pursuant to Part 15 of the FCC Rules. These limits are designed to provide reasonable protection against harmful interference in a residential installation. This equipment generates, uses, and can radiate radio frequency energy and, if not installed and used in accordance with the instructions, may cause harmful interference to radio communications. However, there is no guarantee that interference will not occur in a particular installation. If this equipment does cause harmful interference to radio or television reception, which can be determined by turning the equipment off and on, the user is encouraged to try to correct the interference by one or more of the following measures: Reorient or relocate the receiving antenna. Increase the separation between the equipment and receiver. Connect the equipment into an outlet on a circuit different from that to which the receiver is connected. Consult the dealer or an experienced radio TV technician for help.

Published by Louis Weber, C.E.O., Publications International, Ltd.
7373 North Cicero Avenue
Lincolnwood, Illinois 60712

Ground Floor, 59 Gloucester Place
London W1U 8JJ

Customer Service: 1-888-724-0144 or Customer_Service@pubint.com

www.pilbooks.com

 Publications International, Ltd.

Manufactured in China.

8 7 6 5 4 3 2 1

ISBN-10: 1-60553-920-1
ISBN-13: 978-1-60553-920-1

CONTENTS

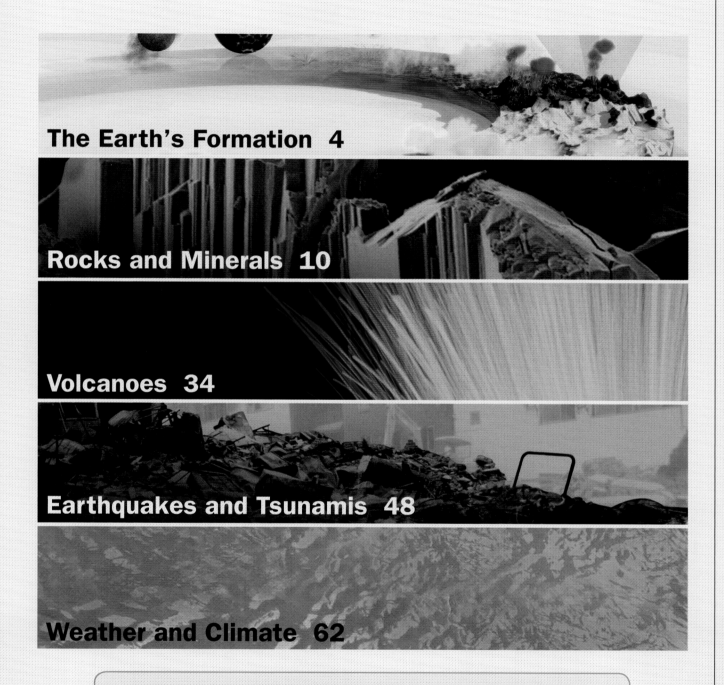

CHANGE THE VOLUME WITH THESE BUTTONS:

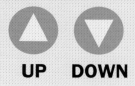

UP   DOWN

The Long History of the Earth

Astronomers suggest that the Earth was formed in the same way and at the same time as the rest of the planets and the Sun. It all began with an immense cloud of helium and hydrogen and a small portion of heavier materials 4.6 billion years ago. Earth emerged from one of these "small" revolving clouds, where the particles constantly collided with one another, producing very high temperatures. Later, a series of processes took place that gave the planet its present shape.

From Chaos to Today's Earth

4.6
BILLION YEARS AGO
FORMATION

Between 4.6 and 4
BILLION YEARS AGO
COOLING

60
MILLION YEARS AGO
FOLDING

542
MILLION YEARS AGO
PALEOZOIC ERA
FRAGMENTATION

1
BILLION YEARS AGO
SUPERCONTINENTS

4
BILLION YEARS AGO
METEORITE COLLISION

3.5
BILLION YEARS AGO
ARCHEAN EON
STABILIZATION

THE AGE OF
SUPER VOLCANOES

The oldest rocks appeared.

When the first crust
cooled, intense volcanic
activity freed gases from the
interior of the planet, and those gases
formed the atmosphere and the oceans.

2.2
BILLION YEARS AGO
WARMING

2.3
BILLION YEARS AGO
"SNOWBALL" EARTH

1.8
BILLION YEARS AGO
PROTEROZOIC ERA

CONTINENTS

The Journey of the Plates

When geophysicist Alfred Wegener suggested in 1910 that the continents were moving, the idea seemed fantastic. Only a half-century later, plate tectonic theory was able to offer an explanation of the phenomenon. Volcanic activity on the ocean floor, *convection currents*, and the melting of rock in the mantle power the continental drift that is still molding the planet's surface today.

Continental Drift

The first ideas on continental drift proposed that the continents floated on the ocean. That idea proved inaccurate. The seven *tectonic plates* contain portions of ocean beds and continents. They drift atop the molten *mantle* like sections of a giant shell.

The Hidden Motor

Convection currents of molten rock propel the crust.

180 MILLION YEARS AGO

LAURASIA

GONDWANA

ANTARCTICA

250 MILLION YEARS AGO

PANGEA

NAZCA PLATE

TONGAN TRENCH

EASTERN PACIFIC RIDGE

PERU-CHILE TRENCH

2 inches
(5 cm)
TYPICAL DISTANCE THE PLATES TRAVEL IN A YEAR

INDO-AUSTRALIAN PLATE

CONVECTION CURRENTS — OUTWARD MOVEMENT

250
Million years
THE NUMBER OF YEARS IT WILL TAKE FOR
THE CONTINENTS TO DRIFT TOGETHER AGAIN

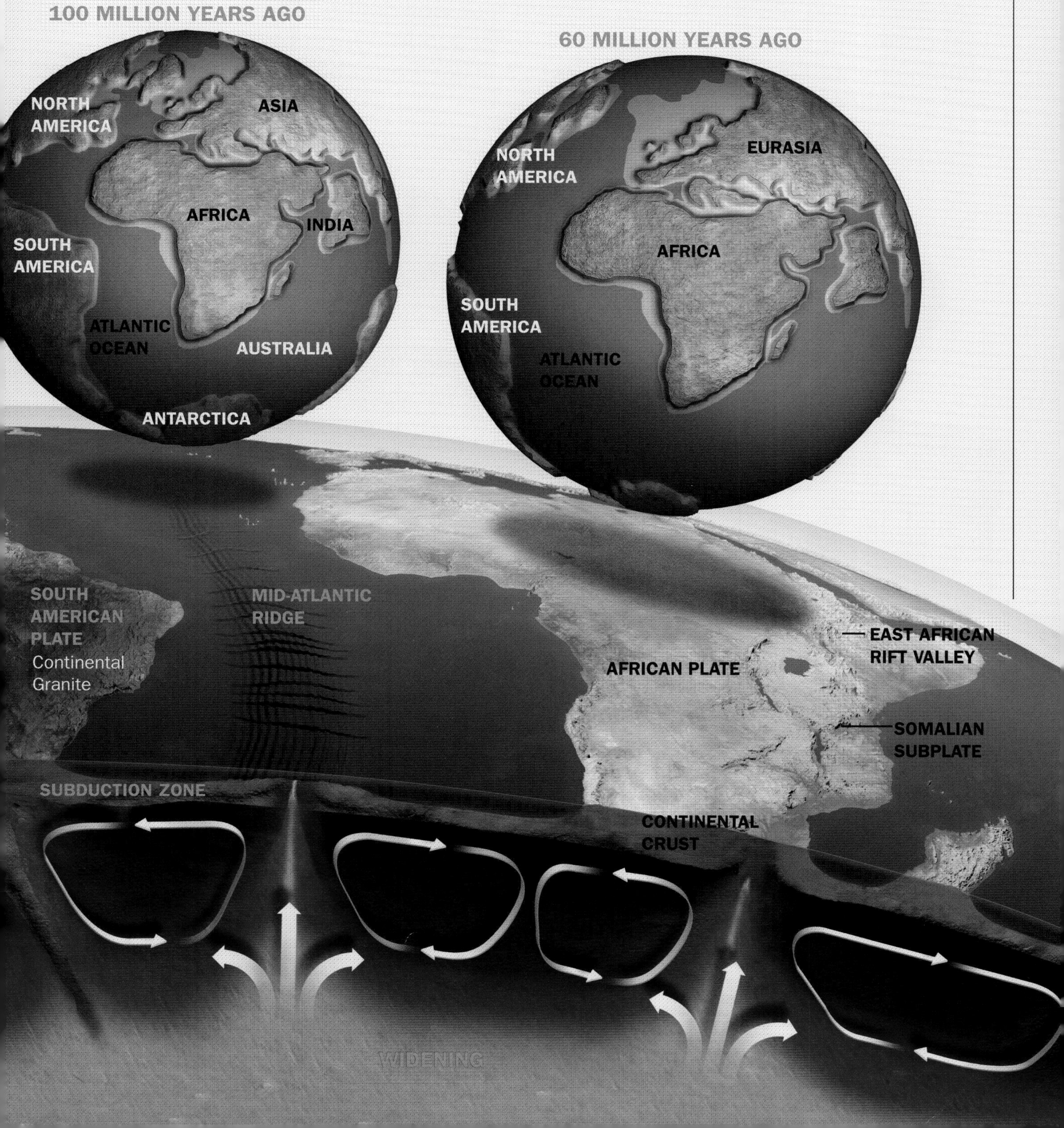

100 MILLION YEARS AGO

NORTH
AMERICA

ASIA

AFRICA

INDIA

SOUTH
AMERICA

ATLANTIC
OCEAN

AUSTRALIA

ANTARCTICA

60 MILLION YEARS AGO

NORTH
AMERICA

EURASIA

AFRICA

SOUTH
AMERICA

ATLANTIC
OCEAN

SOUTH
AMERICAN
PLATE
Continental
Granite

MID-ATLANTIC
RIDGE

AFRICAN PLATE

EAST AFRICAN
RIFT VALLEY

SOMALIAN
SUBPLATE

CONTINENTAL
CRUST

SUBDUCTION ZONE

WIDENING

Stacked Layers

Every 110 feet (33 m) below the Earth's surface, the temperature increases by 1.8 degrees Fahrenheit (1 degree Celsius). To reach the Earth's center, a person would have to burrow through four well-defined layers. The gases that cover the Earth's surface are also divided into layers with different compositions. Forces act on the Earth's crust from above and below to sculpt and permanently alter it.

Earth's Crust

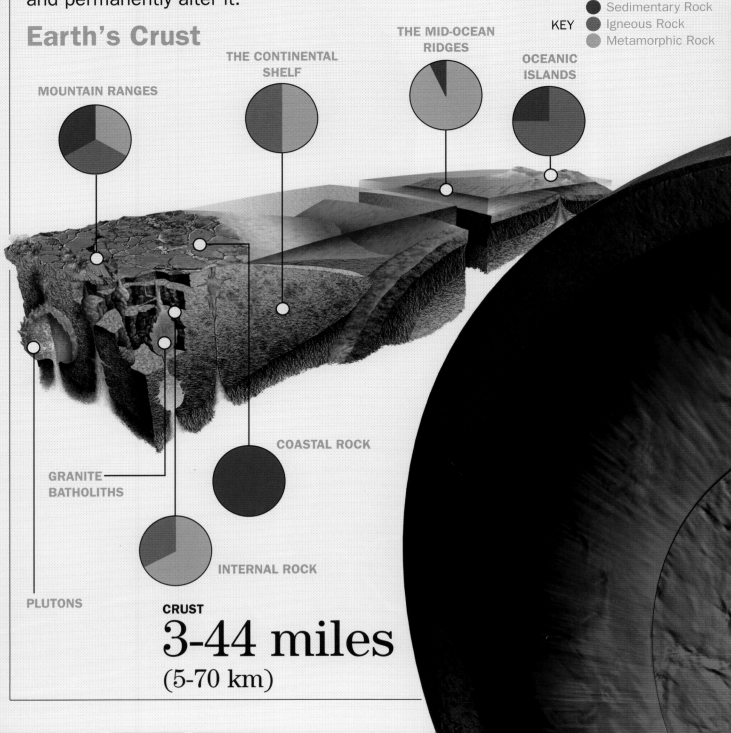

KEY
- Sedimentary Rock
- Igneous Rock
- Metamorphic Rock

THE MID-OCEAN RIDGES

THE CONTINENTAL SHELF

OCEANIC ISLANDS

MOUNTAIN RANGES

COASTAL ROCK

GRANITE BATHOLITHS

INTERNAL ROCK

PLUTONS

CRUST
3-44 miles
(5-70 km)

The Gaseous Envelope

The air and most of the weather events
that affect our lives occur only in the lower
layer of the Earth's atmosphere.

Less than
6 miles
(10 km)
TROPOSPHERE

Less than
31 miles
(50 km)
STRATOSPHERE

Less than
62 miles
(100 km)
MESOSPHERE

Less than
310 miles
(500 km)
THERMOSPHERE

Greater than
310 miles
(500 km)
EXOSPHERE

UPPER MANTLE
370 miles
(600 km)

LITHOSPHERE

LOWER MANTLE
1,430 miles
(2,300 km)

OUTER CORE
1,410 miles
(2,270 km)

ASTHENOSPHERE

INNER CORE
756 miles
(1,216 km)

Before Rock, Mineral

The planet on which we live can be seen as a large rock or, more precisely, as a large sphere composed of many types of rocks. These rocks are composed of tiny fragments of one or more materials.

QUARTZ

MICA

FELDSPAR

GRANITE

CHANGE OF STATE

TORRES DEL PAINE
Chilean Patagonia
Latitude 52° 20´ S
Longitude 71° 55´ W

Composition	**Granite**
Highest Summit	**Paine Grande (10,000 feet [3,050m])**
Surface	**598 acres (242 ha)**

You Are What You Have

Minerals are the "bricks" of materials that make up the Earth and all other solid bodies in the universe. Studying minerals helps us to understand the origin of the Earth. Minerals are classified according to their composition and internal structure, as well as by the properties of hardness, weight, color, *luster*, and transparency.

Components

1 NATIVE MINERALS

A - METALS AND INTERMETALS
B - SEMIMETALS
C - NONMETALS

**MINERALS
COME FROM**
112
elements
listed in the periodic table.

**MORE THAN
4,000
types of minerals**
have been recognized by the International Association of Mineralogy.

SILVER

GOLD

BISMUTH

SULFUR

2 COMPOUND MINERALS

HALITE

A Question of Style

Optical properties involve a mineral's response to the presence of light. This characteristic can be analyzed under a petrographic microscope, which helps determine some of the optical responses of the mineral.

Color

is one of the most striking properties of minerals. However, in determining the identity of a mineral, color is not always useful.

INHERENT COLOR

Some minerals always have the same color.

MALACHITE   **SULFUR**

EXOTIC COLOR

A mineral can have several shades, depending on its impurities or inclusions.

QUARTZ

ROCK CRYSTAL

ROSE

CITRINE

SMOKY

AMETHYST

HEMATITE
Color: Blackish Red to Reddish Gray

Streak Color:
Reddish Brown

AGATE

Luminescence
Certain minerals emit light when they are exposed to particular sources of energy.

Refraction and Luster

METALLIC

SUBMETALLIC

NONMETALLIC

How to Recognize Minerals

A mineral's physical properties are very important for recognizing it at first glance. One physical property is hardness. One mineral is harder than another when the former can scratch the latter. Another physical property of a mineral is its tenacity, or cohesion—that is, its degree of resistance to rupture, deformation, or crushing. Yet another is *magnetism*.

Exfoliation and Fracture

TOURMALINE

COLOR

TYPES OF EXFOLIATION

Cubic

Octahedral

Dodecahedral

Rhombohedral

Prismatic and Pinacoidal

Pinacoidal (Basal)

FRACTURE

IRREGULAR FRACTURE
An uneven, splintery mineral surface

MOHS SCALE

 1 TALC   **2** GYPSUM   **3** CALCITE   **4** FLUORITE   **5** APATITE

DENSITY
reflects the structure
and chemical composition
of a mineral.

 ORTHOCLASE **QUARTZ** **TOPAZ** **CORUNDUM** **DIAMOND**

Precious Crystals

Precious stones are characterized by their beauty, color, transparency, and rarity. Examples are diamonds, emeralds, rubies, and sapphires. Compared to other gems, semiprecious stones are composed of minerals of lesser value. Today diamonds are the most prized gem for their "fire," *luster*, and extreme hardness. The origin of diamonds goes back millions of years, but people began to cut them only in the 14th century. Most diamond deposits are located in South Africa, Namibia, and Australia.

Diamond

② CUTTING AND CARVING

① EXTRACTION

C CARVING

B CUTTING

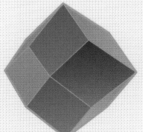
A INSPECTION

Kimberley Mine

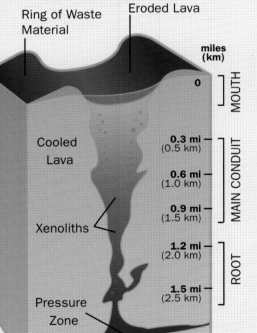

Ring of Waste Material

Eroded Lava

Cooled Lava

Xenoliths

Pressure Zone

miles (km)	
0	MOUTH
0.3 mi (0.5 km)	MAIN CONDUIT
0.6 mi (1.0 km)	
0.9 mi (1.5 km)	
1.2 mi (2.0 km)	ROOT
1.5 mi (2.5 km)	

27.6 tons
(25 metric tons)
of mineral must be removed to obtain a **1 carat diamond.**

1 carat = 0.007 ounce (0.2 grams)

8 carats

0.5 inch (13 mm)

6.5 carats

0.3 inch (6.5 mm)

0.03 carat

0.08 inch (2 mm)

PRECIOUS STONES

Gems

DIAMOND

EMERALD

OPAL

RUBY

③ POLISHING

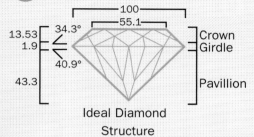

13.53
1.9
43.3

34.3°
40.9°

100
55.1

Crown
Girdle

Pavillion

Ideal Diamond
Structure

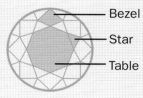

Bezel
Star
Table

BRILLANCE
The internal faces
of the diamond act
as mirrors.

LIGHT

FIRE
Flashes of color
from a well-cut
diamond

LIGHT

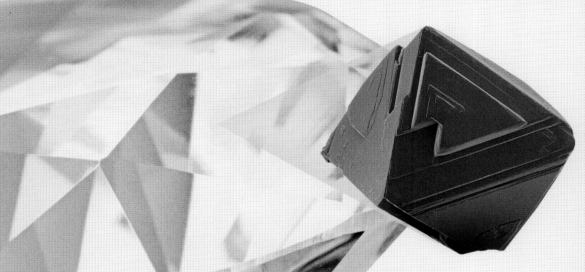

320 microns
(0.32 mm)
MEASURED VERTICALLY

COMMON CUTS

Brilliant   Emerald   Princess   Trillion

Pear   Heart   Oval   Marquise

SEMIPRECIOUS STONES

SAPPHIRE   **TOPAZ**   **AMETHYST**   **GARNET**   **TURQUOISE**

Silicates and Nonsilicates

Silicates, which form 95 percent of the Earth's crust, are the most abundant type of mineral. They are formed of silicon and oxygen. Quartz, olivine, and mica are examples. Nonsilicates are more rare, but they are very important economically. Sulfurs, oxides, sulfates, pure elements, carbonates, hydroxides, and phosphates are all nonsilicates.

Very Few in a Pure State

Native chemical elements are rarely found in the Earth's crust in a pure state.

ASSOCIATION
The greenish color indicates a formation of copper sulfate.

DENDRITES
Microscopic forms that appear when copper solidifies and crystallizes

FORMATION OF CHALOPYRITE
Iron, copper, and sulfur are present.

Copper

Limonite

Apatite

PHOSPHATES

HYDROXIDES

Magnetite

OXIDES

Malachite

HALIDES

CARBONATES

Fluorite

Gypsum Rosette

SULFATES

SULFIDES

0.04 inch
(1 mm)

STRUCTURE OF PYRITE

Pyrite

How to Identify Rocks

Rocks can be classified as *igneous*, *metamorphic*, or *sedimentary* according to the manner in which they were formed. Their specific characteristics depend on the minerals that constitute them. Based on this information, it is possible to know how rocks gained their color, texture, and crystalline structure.

ANGULAR

Shapes

The final shape that a rock acquires depends to a great extent on its resistance to outside forces.

Age

Being able to accurately determine the age of a rock is very useful in the study of geology.

ROUNDED

Mineral Composition

Rocks are natural combinations of two or more minerals.

Color

The color of a rock is determined by the color of the minerals that compose it.

0.4 inch
(1 cm)

Fracture

White Marble
Impurity
White Marble
Pegmatite
White Marble

Texture

refers to the size and arrangement of grains that form a rock.

0.4 inch
(1 cm)

GRAIN
is the size of the individual parts of a rock.

CRYSTALS

Igneous Rocks

Formed from magma or lava, igneous rocks can be classified according to their composition. This classification specially takes into account: the relative proportion of silica, magnesium, and iron minerals found in these type of rocks; their grain size (which reveals how fast they cooled); and their color. Rocks that contain silica, along with much quartz and feldspar, tend to have pale colors; those with low silica content have dark colors created by iron and magnesium-containing minerals. A rock's texture is determined by the configuration of its crystal grains.

Underground: Plutonic or Intrusive Rocks

Rocks of this type formed through the solidification of magma masses deep within other rocks.

GABBRO

MACROPHOTOGRAPHY OF PINK GRANITE

GRANITE

1 mile
(1.6 km)
THE MINIMUM DEPTH AT WHICH GRANITE FORMS

PERIDOTITE

GRANODIORITE

MACROPHOTOGRAPHY OF GRANODIORITE

Dikes and Sills: Rocks Formed in Seams

Some types of igneous rocks are formed from ascending magma that solidifies in seams or fissures. The resulting sheetlike body of rock is called a dike if it has a vertical orientation or a sill if it has a horizontal orientation.

CRYSTAL JOINED BY *VITREOUS* **MASS**

PORPHYRITICS

PEGMATITE IS NATURALLY SMOOTH.

Extrusive Rocks, Products of Volcanoes

Extrusive rocks form through the fast cooling of magma on or near the Earth's surface.

PUMICE

BASALT

GEOMETRIC PRISMS

Hexagon

THE MOST COMMON SHAPE INTO WHICH BASALT CRYSTALLIZES

OBSIDIAN

Organic Rocks

Organic rocks are composed of the remains of living organisms that have undergone processes of *decomposition* and compaction millions of years ago. The change experienced by these substances is called carbonization.

26%

OF THE PRIMARY ENERGY CONSUMED IN THE WORLD COMES FROM COAL.

FORMATION OF PETROLEUM

PETROLEUM TRAPS

Caprock

Storage rock

Anticline

Fault Trap

Stratigraphic Trap

Saline Dome

Key
- Gas
- Petroleum (Oil)
- Water

Coal Formation

LOCATION INSIDE THE EARTH

1 **VEGETATION**

2 **PEAT**

Contains 60% carbon

DEPTH up to 1,000 feet (300 m)

TEMPERATURE up to 77° F (25° C)

③ LIGNITE

Contains **70%** carbon

DEPTH
up to 1,000 to 5,000
feet (300 to 1,500 m)

TEMPERATURE
up to 104° F
(40° C)

④ COAL

Contains **80%** carbon

DEPTH
5,000 to 20,000 feet
(1,500 to 6,000 m)

TEMPERATURE
up to 347° F
(175° C)

⑤ ANTHRACITE

Contains **95%** carbon

DEPTH
20,000 to
25,000 feet
(6,000 to 7,600 m)

TEMPERATURE
up to 572° F
(300° C)

ANTHRACITE
ROCK

WORLD PETROLEUM RESERVES
Billions of barrels

North America
59.5

Europe and Eurasia
140.5

Middle East
742.7

Africa
114.3

Asia Pacific
40.2

Central and
South America
103.5

WORLD COAL RESERVES
Billions of tons

North America
254.4

Europe and Eurasia
287.1

Middle East
0.4

Africa
50.3

Asia Pacific
296.9

Central and
South America
19.9

Common Metamorphic Rocks

The classification of *metamorphic* rocks is not simple because the same conditions of temperature and pressure do not always produce the same final rock. In the face of this difficulty, these rocks are divided into two large groups, taking into account that some exhibit *foliation* and others do not. Most rocks derive their color from the minerals of which they are composed, but their texture depends on more than just their composition.

GARNETIFEROUS SCHIST

SLATE

SLATE MICROGRAPHY

MICACEOUS SCHIST

HORNBLENDE SCHIST

PHYLLITE

Slates and Phyllites

These foliated rocks recrystallized under moderate pressure and temperature conditions.

SLATE

Gneiss

Striped rock that usually contains long and granular minerals. The most common types are quartz, potash, feldspar, and plagioclase.

Stripes

MAKE IT POSSIBLE TO DETERMINE THE DIRECTION IN WHICH PRESSURE WAS EXERTED ON THE ROCK.

Marble and Quartzite

These rocks are compacted and nonfoliated.

GARNETIFEROUS SCHIST

Schist

This rock is more prone to foliation, and it can break off in small sheets.

QUARTZITE

7

IS THE LEVEL OF HARDNESS OF QUARTZITE.

0.04 in (1 mm)

OR MORE: THE SIZE OF MICA GRAINS IN SCHIST— LARGE ENOUGH TO SEE WITH THE UNAIDED EYE

MARBLE

MARBLE MICROGRAPHY

GNEISS

Under Construction

Our planet is not a dead body, complete and unchanging. It is an ever-changing system whose activity we experience all the time: volcanoes erupt, earthquakes occur, and new rocks emerge on the Earth's surface. All these phenomena, which originate in the interior of the planet, are studied in a branch of geology called internal geodynamics. This science analyzes processes that originate with the movement of the crust and result in the raising and sinking of large areas. The movement of the Earth's crust also generates the conditions that form new rocks.

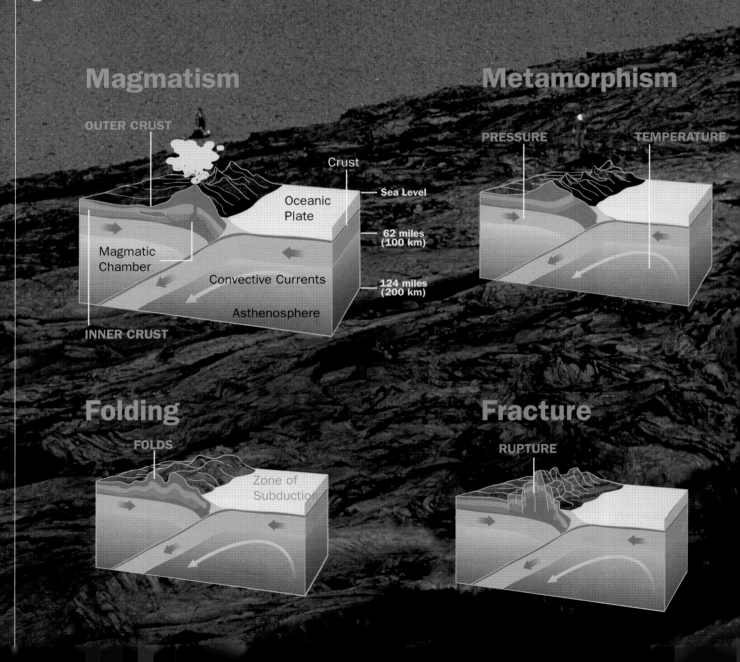

Magmatism

OUTER CRUST

Crust

Sea Level

Oceanic Plate

62 miles (100 km)

Magmatic Chamber

124 miles (200 km)

Convective Currents

Asthenosphere

INNER CRUST

Metamorphism

PRESSURE

TEMPERATURE

Folding

FOLDS

Zone of Subduction

Fracture

RUPTURE

A Changing Surface

The molding of the Earth's crust is the product of two great destructive forces: weathering and erosion. Through the combination of these processes, rocks merge, disintegrate, and join again. Living organisms, especially plant roots and digging animals, cooperate with these geologic processes.

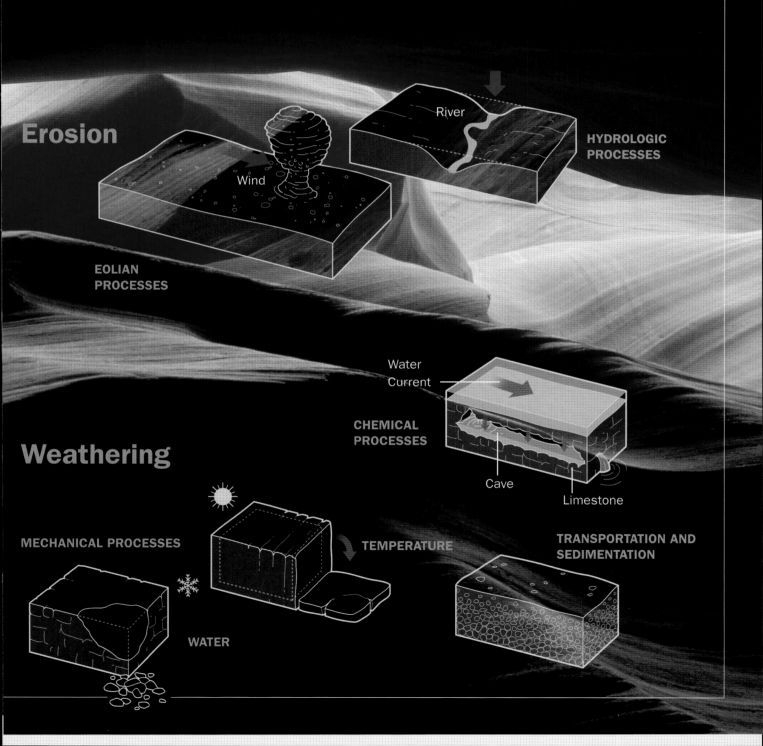

Erosion

Wind

River

HYDROLOGIC PROCESSES

EOLIAN PROCESSES

Water Current

CHEMICAL PROCESSES

Cave

Limestone

Weathering

MECHANICAL PROCESSES

TEMPERATURE

TRANSPORTATION AND SEDIMENTATION

WATER

Flaming Furnace

Volcanoes are among the most powerful
manifestations of our planet's dynamic interior.
The magma they release at the Earth's surface
can cause phenomena that devastate surrounding
areas: explosions, enormous flows of molten rock,
fire and ash that rain from the sky, floods, and
mudslides. Every volcano has a life cycle, during
which it can modify the *topography* and the climate
and after which it becomes extinct.

MOUNTAIN-RANGE VOLCANOES

1 Two plates converge.

2 The rock melts
and forms new
magma.

3 Magma seeps through
cracks in the rocks.

LIFE AND DEATH OF A VOLCANO:
THE FORMATION OF A CALDERA

1 EXPLOSIVE
ERUPTIONS

2 A VOID IS LEFT

ERUPTION OF LAVA

CLOUD OF ASH

STREAMS OF LAVA

CRATER

PARASITIC
VOLCANO

SECONDARY
CONDUIT

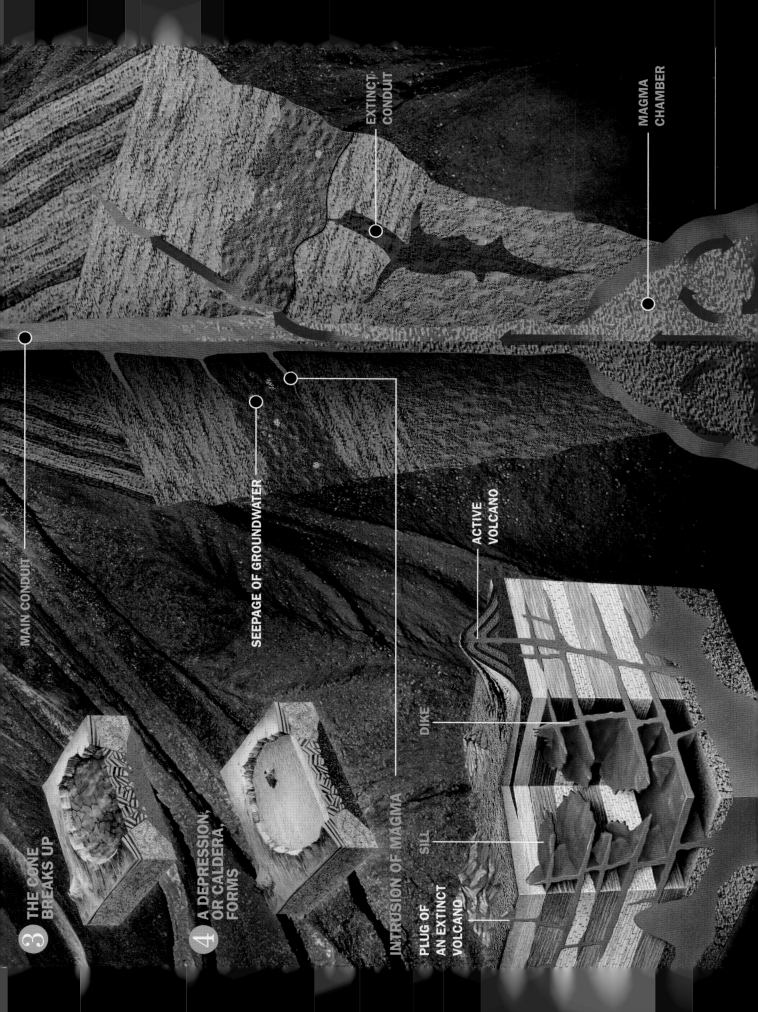

EXTINCT
CONDUIT

MAGMA
CHAMBER

MAIN CONDUIT

SEEPAGE OF GROUNDWATER

ACTIVE
VOLCANO

INTRUSION OF MAGMA

DIKE

SILL

PLUG OF
AN EXTINCT
VOLCANO

3 THE CONE
BREAKS UP

4 A DEPRESSION,
OR CALDERA,
FORMS

Classification

No two volcanoes on Earth are exactly alike, although they have characteristics that permit them to be studied according to six basic types: shield volcanoes, cinder cones, stratovolcanoes, lava cones, fissure volcanoes, and calderas. A volcano's shape depends on its origin, how the eruption began, processes that accompany the volcanic activity, and the degree of danger the volcano poses to life in surrounding areas.

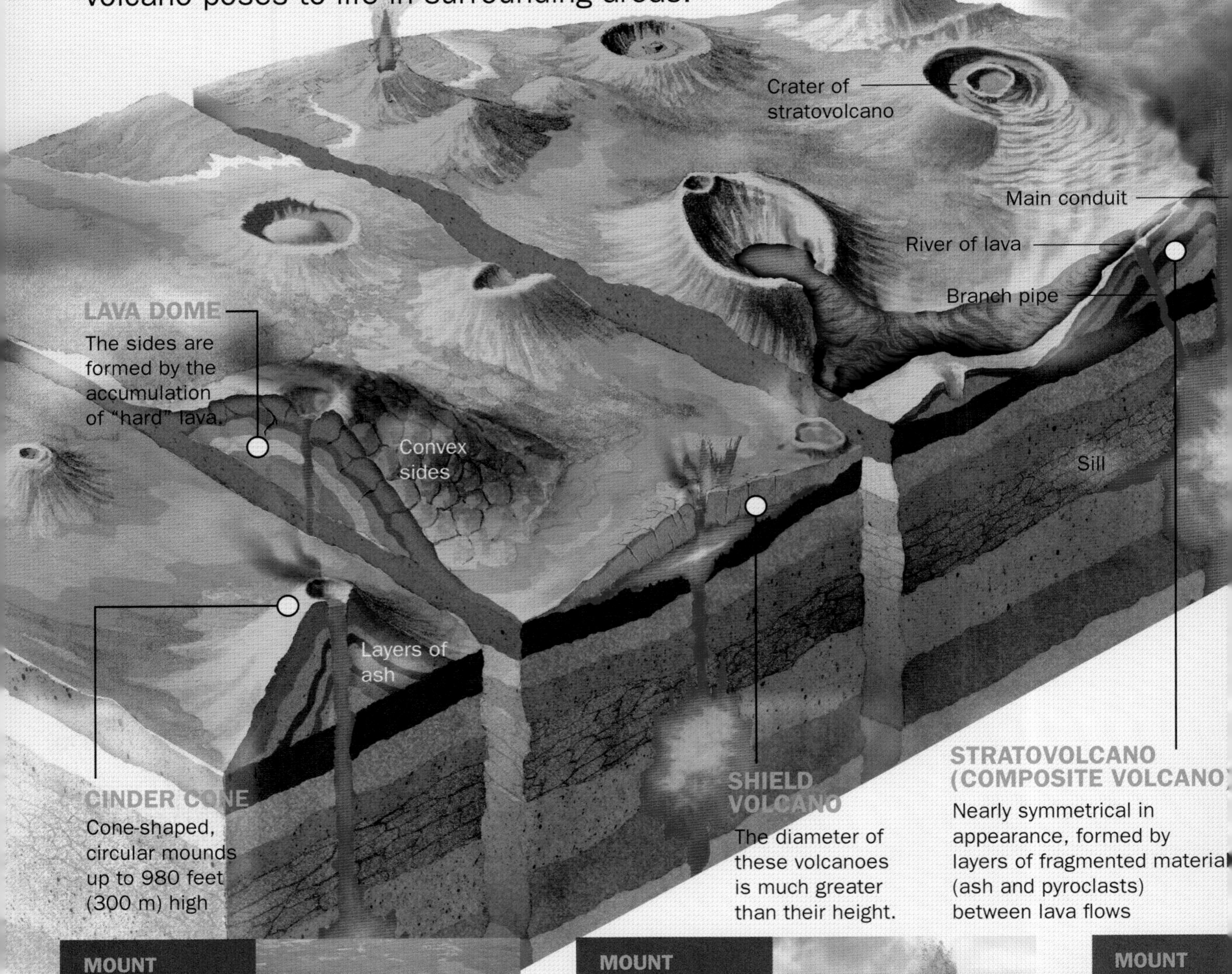
Crater of stratovolcano
Main conduit
River of lava
Branch pipe
Sill
Convex sides
Layers of ash
LAVA DOME
The sides are formed by the accumulation of "hard" lava.
CINDER CONE
Cone-shaped, circular mounds up to 980 feet (300 m) high
SHIELD VOLCANO
The diameter of these volcanoes is much greater than their height.
STRATOVOLCANO (COMPOSITE VOLCANO)
Nearly symmetrical in appearance, formed by layers of fragmented material (ash and pyroclasts) between lava flows

MOUNT ILAMATEPEC
Cinder cone

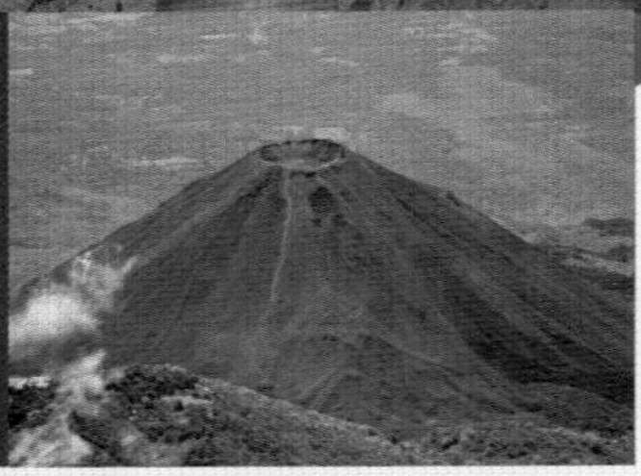

MOUNT KILAUEA
Shield volcano

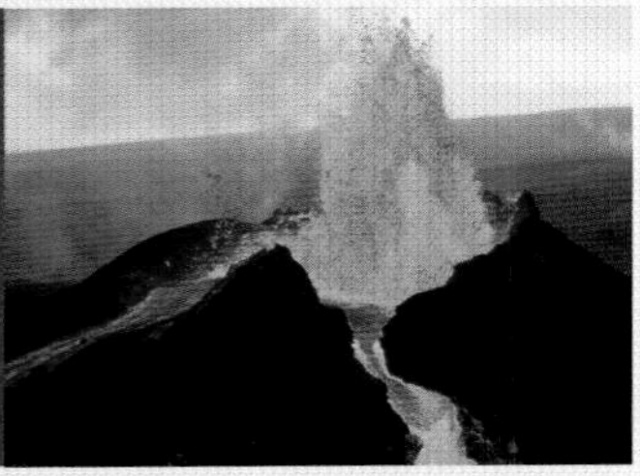

MOUNT FUJI
Composite volcano

IGNEOUS INTRUSIONS: A PECULIAR PROFILE

1 FORMATION OF THE VOLCANIC PLUG

2 INITIAL EROSION

3 THE NECK FORMS

Extinct volcano

Erosion of the cone

Plug of extinct volcano

CHAPEL OF ST. MICHAEL
Built on top of a volcanic neck of hard rock that once sealed the conduit of a volcano

Caldera that contains a lake

Parasitic volcano

Formation of new cone

Shock wave

Lava slope

Magma chamber

CALDERA VOLCANO
Large basins similar to craters but greater than 0.6 mile (1 km) across are called calderas.

Dike

FISSURE VOLCANO
Long, narrow openings found mainly in mid-ocean ridges

CALDERA BLANCA
Caldera volcano

MAUNA ULU
Fissure volcano

Flash of Fire

A volcanic eruption can last from a few hours to several decades. Some are devastating, but others are mild. The severity of the eruption depends on the dynamics between the magma, dissolved gas, and rocks within the volcano. The most potent explosions often result from thousands of years of accumulation of magma and gas, as pressure builds up inside the chamber. Other volcanoes reach an explosive point every few months and have frequent emissions.

Ash

Lapilli

Bomb

3 THE ESCAPE

These materials are ejected.

4 PYROCLASTIC PRODUCTS

In addition to lava, an eruption can eject solid materials called pyroclasts.

Bomb	**2.5 inches (64 mm) and up**
Lapilli	**0.08 to 2.5 inches (2 mm to 64 mm)**
Ash	**Up to 0.08 inch (2 mm)**

Water vapor

Crater

2 IN THE CONDUIT

A solid layer of fragmented materials blocks the magma that contains the volatile gases.

Conduit

5 LAVA FLOWS

Gas particles

Molten rock

1 IN THE CHAMBER

Rising magma, under pressure, mixes with gases in the ground.

EFFUSIVE ACTIVITY

Mild eruptions with a low frequency of explosions

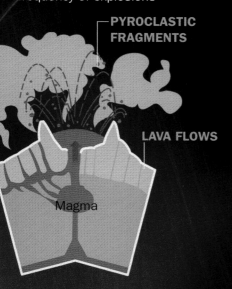

PYROCLASTIC FRAGMENTS

LAVA FLOWS

Magma

EXPLOSIVE ACTIVITY

Comes from the combination of high levels of gas with relatively viscous lava, which can produce pyroclasts and build up high pressure.

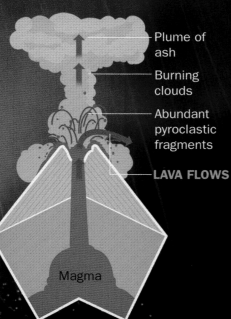

Plume of ash

Burning clouds

Abundant pyroclastic fragments

LAVA FLOWS

Magma

TYPES OF EFFUSIVE ERUPTION

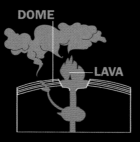

DOME

LAVA

FISSURE

LAVA

HAWAIIAN
Volcanoes such as Mauna Loa and Kilauea expel large amounts of basaltic lava with a low gas content.

FISSURE
Typical in ocean rift zones

TYPES OF EXPLOSIVE ERUPTION

Cloud of burning material from about **330 to 3,300 feet (100-1,000 m)** high

Lava flow

The column can reach a height of **49,000 feet (15 km)**

Cloud can reach above **82,000 feet (25 km)**

Burning cloud moving down the slope

Lava plug

STROMBOLIAN   **VULCANIAN**   **VESUVIAN**   **PELEAN**

FROM OUTER SPACE

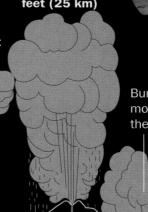

Volcanic ash

Snow and ice

Lava flow

LAVA FLOW MT. KILAUEA, HAWAII

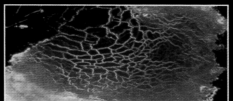

LAKE OF LAVA MAKA-O-PUHL, HAWAII

COOLED LAVA (PAHOEHOE) MT. KILAUEA, HAWAII

Latent Danger

Some locations have a greater propensity for volcanic activity. Most of these areas are found where tectonic plates meet, whether they are approaching or moving away from each other. The largest concentration of volcanoes is found in a region of the Pacific known as the "Ring of Fire." Volcanoes are also found in the Mediterranean Sea, in Africa, and in the Atlantic Ocean.

Arctic Ocean

NOVARUPTA, ALASKA, U.S.

MOUNT ST. HELENS, WASHINGTON, U.S.

AVACHINSKY, RUSSIA

FUJIYAMA, JAPAN

Asia

MAUNA LOA, HAWAII, U.S.

KILAUEA, HAWAII, U.S.

PINATUBO, PHILIPPINES

The Pacific "Ring of Fire"

Formed by the edges of the Pacific tectonic plate, where most of the world's volcanoes are found.

Oceania

KRAKATOA, INDONESIA

TAMBORA, INDONESIA

Indian Ocean

Pacific Ocean

EAST EPI, VANUATU

AUSTRALIAN PLATE

PACIFIC PLATE

The Tallest

	Ojos del Salado, Chile/Argentina 22,595 ft (6,887 m)	Llullaillaco, Chile/Argentina 22,110 ft (6,739 m)	Tipas, Argentina 21,850 ft (6,660 m)	Incahuasi, Chile/Argentina 21,720 ft (6,621 m)	Sajama, Bolivia 21,460 ft (6,542 m)	Mauna Loa, Hawaii Shield volcano 13,680 ft (4,170 m) above sea level

SEA LEVEL

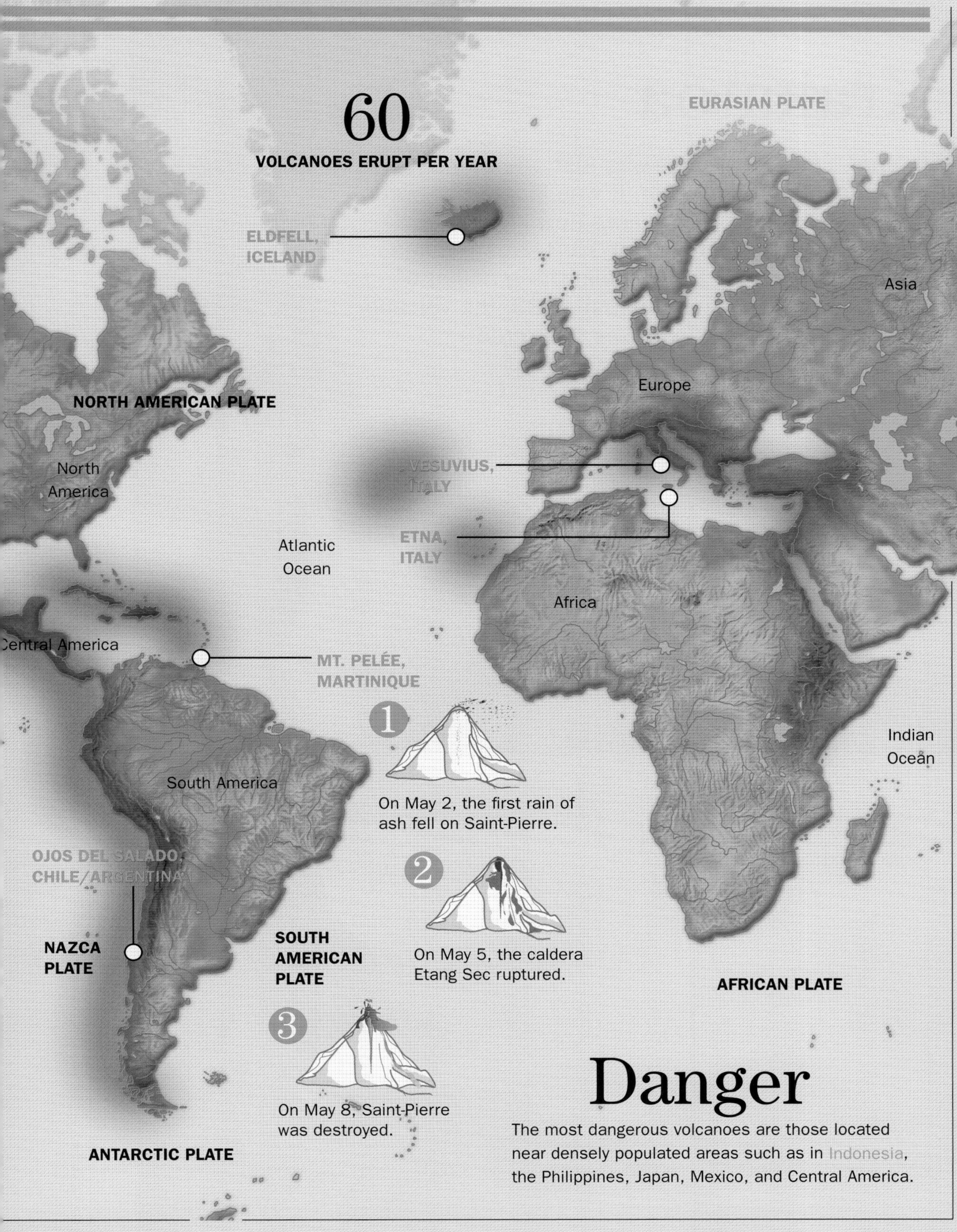

60
VOLCANOES ERUPT PER YEAR

EURASIAN PLATE

Asia

Europe

ELDFELL,
ICELAND

NORTH AMERICAN PLATE

North
America

Atlantic
Ocean

VESUVIUS,
ITALY

ETNA,
ITALY

Africa

Central America

MT. PELÉE,
MARTINIQUE

Indian
Ocean

① On May 2, the first rain of
ash fell on Saint-Pierre.

South America

② On May 5, the caldera
Etang Sec ruptured.

OJOS DEL SALADO,
CHILE/ARGENTINA

SOUTH
AMERICAN
PLATE

AFRICAN PLATE

NAZCA
PLATE

③ On May 8, Saint-Pierre
was destroyed.

ANTARCTIC PLATE

Danger
The most dangerous volcanoes are those located
near densely populated areas such as in Indonesia,
the Philippines, Japan, Mexico, and Central America.

Krakatoa

In early 1883, Krakatoa was just one of many volcanic islands on Earth. It was located between Java and Sumatra in the area now known as Indonesia. It had an area of 10.8 square miles (28 sq km) and a central peak with a height of 2,690 feet (820 m). In August 1883, the volcano exploded, and the island was shattered.

The Island That Exploded

Krakatoa was near the subduction zone between the Indo-Australian and Eurasian plates. The island's inhabitants were unconcerned about the volcano because the most recent previous eruption had been in 1681. Some even thought the volcano was extinct.

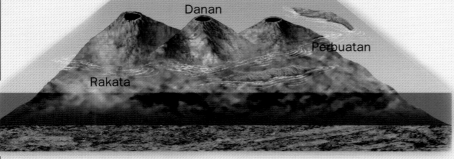

Danan
Perbuatan
Rakata

 **BEFORE**

In May the volcano began showing signs in the form of small quakes and spouting vapor, smoke, and ash.

 DURING

At 5:30 a.m. the island burst from the accumulated pressure.

34 miles (55 km)

The height of the column of ash

130 feet (40 m)

The height of the tsunami waves

KRAKATOA
Latitude 6° 06´ S
Longitude 105° 25´ E

Surface Area	**10.8 square miles (28 sq km)**
Remaining Surface Area	**3 square miles (8 sq km)**
Range of the Explosion	**2,900 miles (4,600 km)**
Range of Debris	**1,550 miles (2,500 km)**
Tsunami Victims	**36,000**

RAKATA — Crater's edge — ANAK KRAKATOA

Panjang

Sertung

PYROCLASTICS

3 AFTER

A crater nearly 4 miles (6.4 km) in diameter
was left where the volcano had been.

Aftereffects

The ash released into the atmosphere left
enough particles suspended in the air to give the
Moon a blue tinge for years afterward.

LONG-TERM EFFECTS

WATER LEVEL   PRESSURE WAVE

Stratosphere

English Channel

Madagascar

ATMOSPHERE

500 megatons

THE ENERGY RELEASED

Precision Instruments

The destructive potential of earthquakes gave rise to the need to study, measure, and record them. Earthquake records, called "seismograms," are produced by instruments called "seismographs," which basically capture the oscillations of a mass and transform them into signals that can be measured and recorded. An earthquake is usually analyzed by means of three seismographs. One seismograph detects the vibrations produced from north to south, another records those from east to west, and a third detects vertical vibrations, those that go up and down.

Seismometers in History

Modern seismometers have digital mechanisms that provide maximum precision. The sensors are still based on seismic energy moving a mechanical part, however, and that is essentially the same principle that operated the first instrument used to evaluate earthquakes.

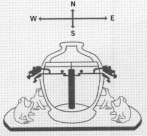

HOW IT WORKS
The oscillating mass vibrates when an earthquake takes place.

Seismic Wave

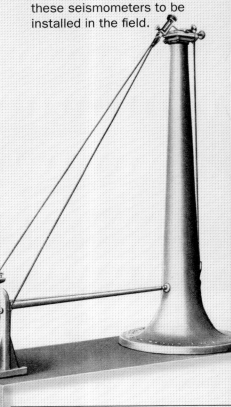

1950
PORTABLE SEISMOMETER
Their strong structure allowed these seismometers to be installed in the field.

123
HENG'S SEISMOSCOPE
The first known seismometer was invented by Chinese mathematician *Zhang Heng*.

1906
BOSCH-OMORI SEISMOMETER
A horizontal pendulum with a pen that makes a mark directly on a paper roll.

1980
WILMORE PORTABLE SEISMOMETER
A sensitive mass vibrates and moves to the rhythm of the seismic energy inside the tube-shaped mechanism.

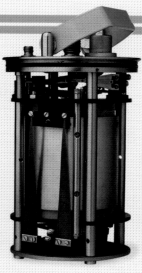

Pioneers of Seismology

ROBERT MALLET

JOHN MILNE

RICHARD OLDHAM

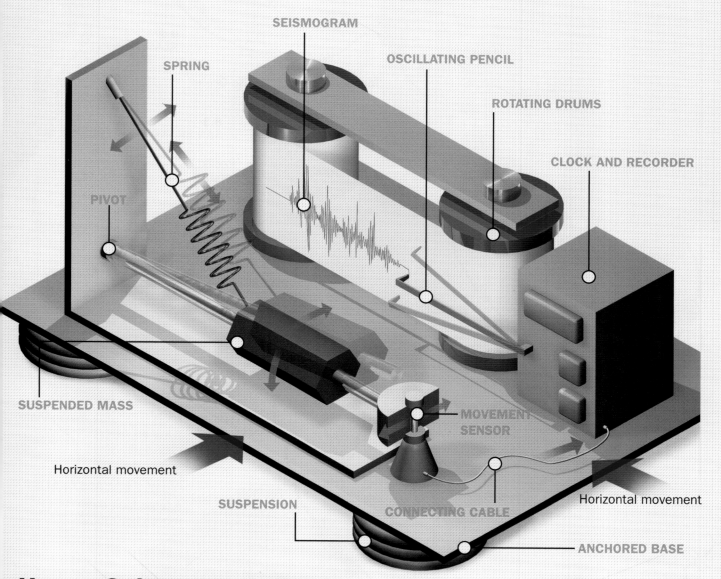

SEISMOGRAM

OSCILLATING PENCIL

ROTATING DRUMS

CLOCK AND RECORDER

SPRING

PIVOT

SUSPENDED MASS

Horizontal movement

SUSPENSION

MOVEMENT SENSOR

CONNECTING CABLE

Horizontal movement

ANCHORED BASE

How a Seismograph Works
The Earth's tremors produce movements in the mass that serves as a sensor. These movements are transformed into electric or digital signals to give versatility in processing and recording the data.

Historic Earthquakes

The Earth is alive. It moves, it shifts, it crashes and quakes, and it has done so since its origin. Earthquakes vary from a soft vibration to violent and terrorizing movements. Many earthquakes have gone down in history as the worst natural catastrophes ever survived by humanity.

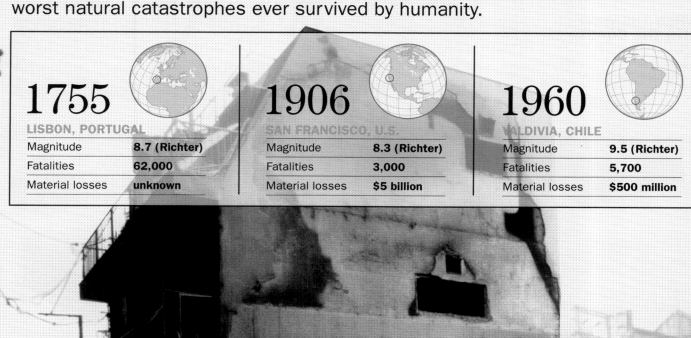

1755
LISBON, PORTUGAL

Magnitude	**8.7 (Richter)**
Fatalities	**62,000**
Material losses	**unknown**

1906
SAN FRANCISCO, U.S.

Magnitude	**8.3 (Richter)**
Fatalities	**3,000**
Material losses	**$5 billion**

1960
VALDIVIA, CHILE

Magnitude	**9.5 (Richter)**
Fatalities	**5,700**
Material losses	**$500 million**

KOBE, JAPAN

1985

MEXICO CITY, MEXICO

Magnitude	8.1 (Richter)
Fatalities	11,000
Material losses	$1 billion

1995

KOBE, JAPAN

Magnitude	6.8 (Richter)
Fatalities	6,433
Material losses	$100 billion

2004

SUMATRA, INDONESIA

Magnitude	9.0 (Richter)
Fatalities	230,507
Material losses	incalculable

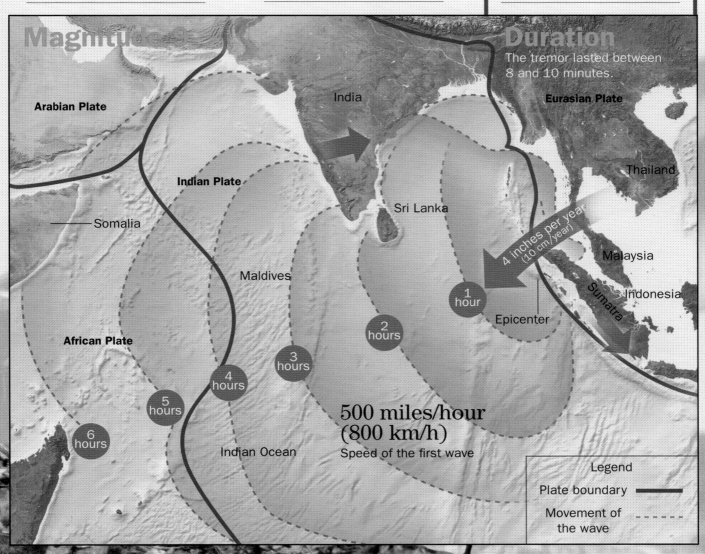

Magnitude

Duration
The tremor lasted between 8 and 10 minutes.

Arabian Plate

India

Eurasian Plate

Indian Plate

Somalia

Sri Lanka

Thailand

4 inches per year (10 cm/year)

Maldives

Malaysia

Indonesia

Sumatra

1 hour

Epicenter

2 hours

African Plate

3 hours

4 hours

5 hours

6 hours

500 miles/hour (800 km/h)
Speed of the first wave

Indian Ocean

Legend
Plate boundary ———
Movement of the wave – – – –

2005

KASHMIR, PAKISTAN

Magnitude	7.6 (Richter)
Fatalities	80,000
Material losses	$595 million

2010

LÉOGÂNE, HAITI

Magnitude	7.0 (Richter)
Fatalities	over 200,000
Material losses	Billions

2010

CENTRAL CHILE

Magnitude	8.8 (Richter)
Fatalities	over 700
Material losses	Billions

T F

Pure Air

The atmosphere is the mass of air that envelops the surface of the Earth. It regulates the quantity and type of solar energy that reaches the surface of the Earth. The atmosphere, in turn, absorbs energy radiated by the crust of the Earth, the polar ice caps and the oceans, and other surfaces on the planet.

GASES IN THE AIR

Carbon dioxide
0.04%

Other gases
0.03%

Argon
0.93%

Oxygen
21%

Nitrogen
78%

DISTANT ORBIT

GREENHOUSE EFFECT

Produced by the absorption of infrared emissions by the greenhouse gases in the atmosphere.

MILITARY SATELLITES

METEORS

EXOSPHERE

The upper limit of the atmosphere

AURORAS

6%

of solar radiation is reflected by the atmosphere.

THERMOSPHERE

Found between an altitude of 55 and 300 miles (90-500 km)

ROCKET
PROBES

MESOSPHERE

Located between an
altitude of 30 to 55
miles (50-90 km), it
absorbs very little
energy yet emits a
large amount of it.

COSMIC RAYS

Noctilucent clouds
The only clouds
that exist above
the troposphere

Solar Radiation

STRATOSPHERE

Extends from an altitude
of 6 miles to 30 miles
(10-50 km).

THE OZONE LAYER

COMMERCIAL FLIGHTS

Tropical
storm
clouds

TROPOSPHERE

Starts at sea level and goes to an altitude
of six miles (10 km). It provides conditions
suitable for life to exist.

HIGH MOUNTAINS

Cirrus

Capricious Forms

Clouds are masses of large drops of water and ice crystals. They form because the water vapor contained in the air condenses or freezes as it rises through the troposphere. How the clouds develop depends on the altitude and the velocity of the rising air. Cloud shapes are divided into three basic types: cirrus, cumulus, and stratus. They are also classified as high, medium, and low depending on the altitude they reach above sea level.

TYPES OF CLOUDS

CIRRUS

CUMULUS

STRATUS

NIMBUS

Exosphere

300 miles (500 km)

50 miles (90 km)

Mesosphere

Stratosphere

30 miles (50 km)

6 miles (10 km)

Troposphere

HOW THEY ARE FORMED

Clouds are formed when the rising air cools to the point where it cannot hold the water vapor it contains. In such a circumstance, the air is said to be saturated, and the excess water vapor condenses.

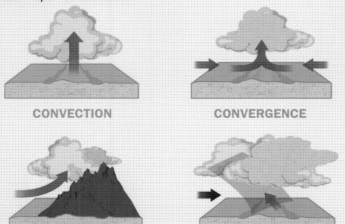

CONVECTION

CONVERGENCE

GEOGRAPHIC ELEVATION

PRESENCE OF A FRONT

T R O

6 miles (10 km)

-67° F (-55° C)

HIGH CLOUDS

CIRROSTRATUS
A very extensive cloud that eventually covers the whole sky

2.5 miles (4 km)

14° F (-10° C)

MEDIUM CLOUDS

CUMULONIMBUS
A storm cloud

50° F (10° C)

1.2 miles (2 km)

CUMULUS
A cloud that is generally dense with well-defined outlines

LOW CLOUDS

59° F (15° C)

0 miles (0 km)

HERE

CIRRUS
A high, thin cloud

CIRROCUMULUS
A cloud formation composed of very small, granulated elements

ALTOCUMULUS
A formation of rounded clouds in groups

ALTOSTRATUS
Large, nebulous, compact, uniform, slightly layered masses

STRATOCUMULUS
A cloud that is horizontal and very long

NIMBOSTRATUS
Brings rain or snow

STRATUS
A large cloud that extends over a large area

by the vehicle.

The Inside

The altitude at which clouds are formed depends on the stability of the air and the humidity. The highest and coldest clouds have ice crystals. The lowest and warmest clouds have drops of water.

1.2 to 5 miles
(2-8 km)
Thickness of a storm cloud

150,000 tons of water
can be contained in a storm cloud.

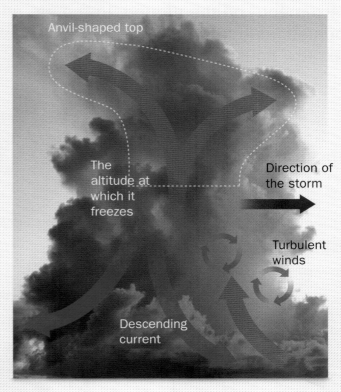

Anvil-shaped top

The altitude at which it freezes

Direction of the storm

Turbulent winds

Descending current

Waves

Lines of cumulus clouds

Wind

Mild winds

Lenticular cloud

Rotating cloud

SPECIAL FORMATIONS

CLOUD STREETS
Light winds usually produce lines of cumulus clouds positioned as if along streets.

LENTICULAR CLOUDS
Lenticular clouds are formed near mountains.

Monsoons

The strong humid winds that usually affect the tropical zone are called monsoons, an Arabic word meaning "seasonal winds." During summer in the Northern Hemisphere, they blow across Southeast Asia, especially the Indian peninsula. Conditions change in the winter, and the winds reverse and shift toward the northern regions of Australia. This phenomenon can cause heavy rains and flooding.

UNDERWATER HARVEST
The mud increases the fertility of the soil.

THERMAL DIFFERENCE BETWEEN THE LAND AND THE OCEAN

THE LAND IS COLD

THE SEA IS A LITTLE WARMER THAN THE LAND

THE EARTH IS HOT

THE SEA IS COLD

AREAS AFFECTED BY MONSOONS

THE MONSOON CAUSES
OVERFLOWING RIVERS

Wa
hu

Co
dry

PA
Nor
pat
16(
(50

FU
It c
tor
acc
da
by

Hurricanes

A *hurricane*, with its ferocious winds, banks of clouds, and torrential rains, is the most spectacular meteorological phenomenon of the Earth's weather. It is characterized by an intense low-pressure center surrounded by cloud bands arranged in spiral form; these rotate around the eye of the hurricane in a clockwise direction in the Southern Hemisphere and in the opposite direction in the Northern Hemisphere. While tornadoes are brief and relatively limited, hurricanes are enormous and slow-moving, and their passage usually takes many lives.

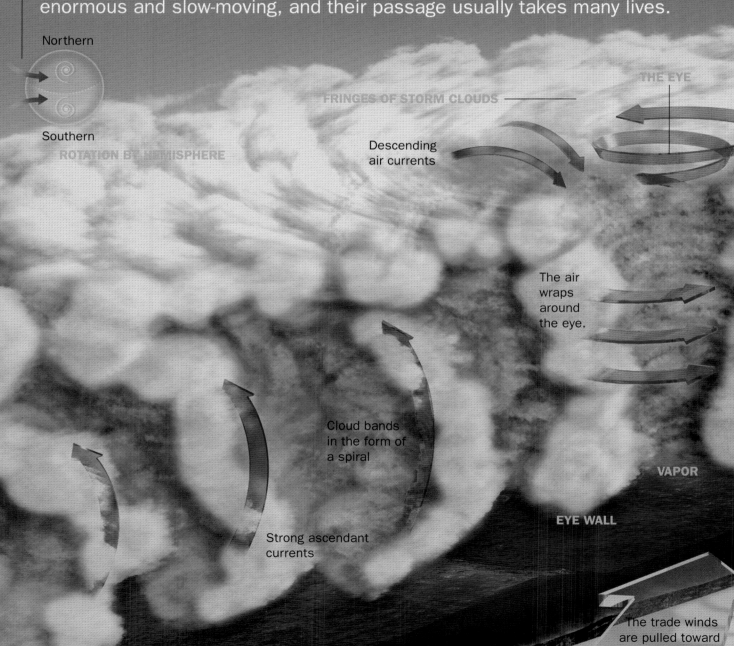

Northern

Southern

ROTATION BY HEMISPHERE

FRINGES OF STORM CLOUDS

THE EYE

Descending
air currents

The air
wraps
around
the eye.

Cloud bands
in the form of
a spiral

VAPOR

EYE WALL

Strong ascendant
currents

The trade winds
are pulled toward
the storm.

DAY 1

DAY 2

DAY 3

Hurricane Typhoon

DANGER ZONE

Cyclone

DAY 6

DAY 12

1 BIRTH
Forms over warm seas.

2 DEVELOPMENT
Begins to ascend.

FRICTION

19 miles per hour (30 km/h)
Velocity at which it approaches the coast

3 DEATH
They pass from the sea to the land.

The high-wind altitude winds blow from outside the storm.

Path of the hurricane

92 feet (28 m)
Maximum height reached by the waves

1
2
3
4
5

WIND ACTIVITY

CLASSIFICATION OF DAMAGE DONE
Saffir-Simpson category

	Damage	Speed miles per hour (km/h)
CLASS 1	minimum	74 to 95 (119 to 153)
CLASS 2	moderate	96 to 110 (154 to 177)
CLASS 3	extensive	111 to 130 (178 to 209)
CLASS 4	extreme	131 to 155 (210 to 250)
CLASS 5	catastrophic	more than 155 (250)

Climate Zones

Different places in the world, even if far removed from each other, can be grouped into climate zones—that is, into regions that have similar climatic elements, such as temperature, pressure, rain, and humidity. There is some disagreement about the number and description of each of these regions, but the illustrations given on this map are generally accepted.

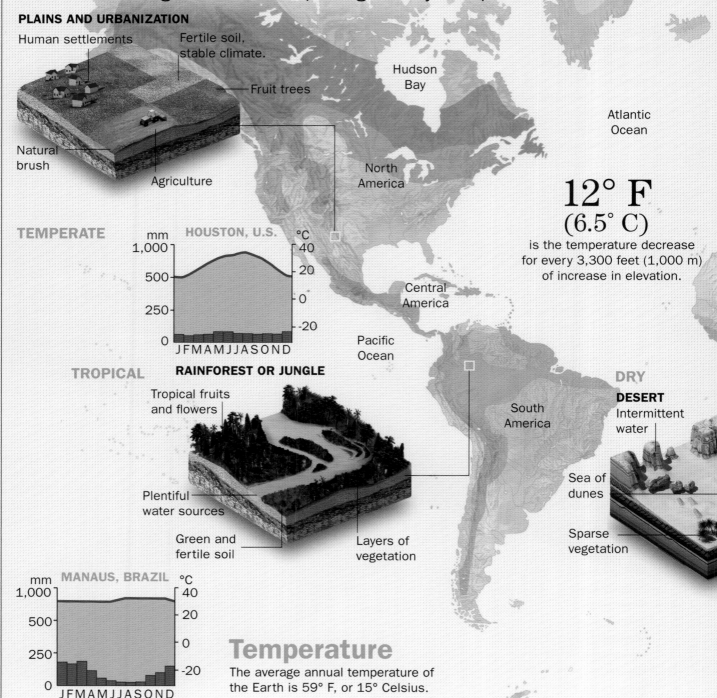

PLAINS AND URBANIZATION

Human settlements

Fertile soil, stable climate.

Fruit trees

Natural brush

Agriculture

Ice cap

Hudson Bay

Atlantic Ocean

North America

TEMPERATE

mm   HOUSTON, U.S.   °C
1,000   40
                          20
500
                          0
250
                          -20
0
J F M A M J J A S O N D

12° F
(6.5° C)
is the temperature decrease for every 3,300 feet (1,000 m) of increase in elevation.

Central America

Pacific Ocean

TROPICAL

RAINFOREST OR JUNGLE

Tropical fruits and flowers

Plentiful water sources

Green and fertile soil

Layers of vegetation

South America

DRY

DESERT

Intermittent water

Sea of dunes

Sparse vegetation

mm   MANAUS, BRAZIL   °C
1,000   40
                           20
500
                           0
250
                           -20
0
J F M A M J J A S O N D

Temperature
The average annual temperature of the Earth is 59° F, or 15° Celsius.

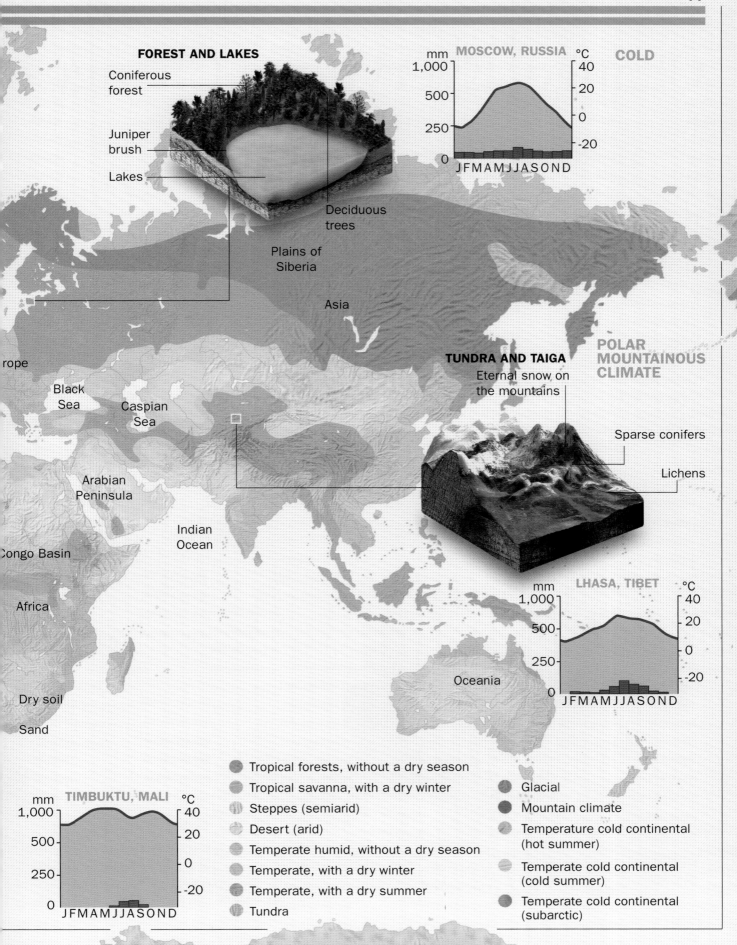

FOREST AND LAKES

Coniferous forest

Juniper brush

Lakes

Deciduous trees

Plains of Siberia

Asia

rope

Black Sea

Caspian Sea

Arabian Peninsula

Indian Ocean

Congo Basin

Africa

Dry soil

Sand

MOSCOW, RUSSIA

mm   °C
1,000   40
500   20
250   0
              -20
0
J F M A M J J A S O N D

COLD

TUNDRA AND TAIGA

Eternal snow on the mountains

POLAR MOUNTAINOUS CLIMATE

Sparse conifers

Lichens

LHASA, TIBET

mm   °C
1,000   40
              20
500
250   0
              -20
0
J F M A M J J A S O N D

Oceania

TIMBUKTU, MALI

mm   °C
1,000   40
              20
500
250   0
              -20
0
J F M A M J J A S O N D

- Tropical forests, without a dry season
- Tropical savanna, with a dry winter
- Steppes (semiarid)
- Desert (arid)
- Temperate humid, without a dry season
- Temperate, with a dry winter
- Temperate, with a dry summer
- Tundra

- Glacial
- Mountain climate
- Temperature cold continental (hot summer)
- Temperate cold continental (cold summer)
- Temperate cold continental (subarctic)

Change, Everything Changes

Atlantic Ocean

North America

The Most Respon

The climate of the planet is constantly changing. At present, the average global temperature is approximately 59° F (15° C). Geologic and other types of evidence suggest that in the past the average could have been as low as 45° F (7° C) and as high as 81° F (27° C). Climate change is, in large part, caused by human activities, which cause an increase in the concentration of *greenhouse gases*.

TEMPERATURES CONTINUE TO RISE

Central America

FROM 3.6° TO 5.6° F (2° TO 3° C)

South America

FROM 1.8° TO 3.6 (1° TO 2° C)

Normal thickness of the ozone layer

The ozone layer stops ultraviolet rays.

Hole in the ozone

Surface of the earth

Rays that pass through the ozone layer

The icy coastline

THINNING OF THE OZONE LAYER
The ozone layer protects us from ultraviolet rays, but, because of the release of artificial substances, it is thinning out.

THE EFFECT OF POLAR MELTING
As ice and snow melt, many of today's coastlines will become submerged under water, which will cause yet more ice to melt.

**MORE THAN 10.8° F
(6° C)**

**FROM 9° TO 10.8° F
(5° TO 6° C)**

**FROM 7.2° TO 9° F
(4° TO 5° C)**

**ROM 5.4° TO 7.2° F
(3° TO 4° C)**

Europe

Asia

Africa

Indian
Ocean

Oceania

Incident rays

Energy is
integrated into the
climatic system.

Long-wave radiation
emitted by the Earth
is trapped by the
atmosphere.

Atmosphere

Surface of
the Earth

ACCELERATION OF THE
GREENHOUSE EFFECT
Ice reflects solar radiation, whereas the
soil of jungles, forests, and steppes
absorbs the energy and radiates it as
sensible heat. This artificially increases
the greenhouse effect and contributes
to global warming.

Cause and Effect
The burning of fossil fuels and the
indiscriminate cutting of *deciduous forests*
and rainforests cause an increase in
the concentration of carbon dioxide,
methane, and other greenhouse
gases. They trap heat and increase
the greenhouse effect.

Solar rays

CO_2 is released

Ocean

Warm marine current

Accelerated Melting

The climate is changing at a disconcerting speed. Glaciers are retreating, and the sea level is rising because of a phenomenon known as thermal expansion. Scientists evaluating the planet's health deduce that this is the consequence of the Earth warming too rapidly. Human activity—in particular, the burning of fossil fuels and the consequent accumulation of greenhouse gases in the atmosphere—has increased this trend.

Why It Happens

The thawing at the poles is, in part, caused by the increase of greenhouse gases.

1. Sunlight reflects from layers of ice.

2. Where the ice is thinnest, or cracked, radiation penetrates to the ocean.

5. Once exposed to the air, the CO_2 is absorbed by the atmosphere.

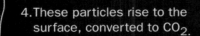
4. These particles rise to the surface, converted to CO_2.

Particles of CO_2

3. Ice absorbs the heat from sunlight and releases a great quantity of trapped carbon particles.

2010-30

2040-60

2070-90

ADVANCING WATERS

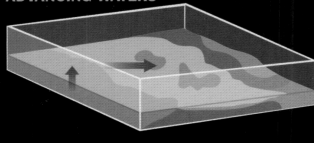

Antarctica

The Antarctic loses 36 cubic miles (152 cu km) of ice per year.